The Me 262 Stormbird Story

The Me 262 Stormbird Story

John Christopher

The History Press

Also in this series:

The Harrier Story
The Hunter Story
The Hurricane Story
The Lancaster Story
The Spitfire Story
The Vulcan Story
The Tornado Story

Half title page:
Side view of Tango-Tango at Bitburg in 2008. (Jean-Marie Spapen)

Page 2: *An Me 262 abandoned in a forest clearing beside the Autobahn.*

Title page: *White 1, two-seater replica seen with a former adversary, the B-17 Super Fortress. (Me 262 Project)*

▶ *Me 262A-1c Tango-Tango in flight. (Jim Larsen)*

Published in the United Kingdom in 2010 by
The History Press
The Mill · Brimscombe Port · Stroud · Gloucestershire · GL5 2QG

Copyright © John Christopher 2010

John Christopher has asserted the moral right to be identified as the author of this work.

British Library Cataloguing in Publication Data
A catalogue record for this book is available from the British Library.

Hardback ISBN 978-0-7524-5303-3

Typesetting and origination by The History Press
Printed in Italy

CONTENTS

➤ *Rare air-to-air photographs, such as this one of an Me 262 attacking an American bomber formation, gave the Allies the first glimpse of what they were up against. (US National Archives)*

55033 A C

I am indebted to the many international sources who have contributed imagery and information for *The Me 262 Stormbird Story*. These include the Australian War Memorial, the German Federal Archives (Bundesarchiv), NASA, the South African National Museum of Military History, Susan Halteman, curator of The Harold F. Pitcairn Wings of Freedom Museum at Willows Grove (Delaware Valley Historic Aircraft Association), the USAF and the National Museum of the US Air Force, the US Navy, the US Department of Defense and Maureen McKnight of Legend Flyers (the Me 262 Project).

A number of dedicated and talented photographers have generously allowed their pictures to be published. These include: Raoul Blignaut and Chantal Smith, Danner Gyde Poulsen, Gryffindor, Jan Honcu, Jim Kershner, Steve Madsen, Andreas Mowinckel, Brenden Sgalio, Ad Meskins, Mark Smith and Jean-Marie Spapen. In particular, I must make special mention of Jim Larsen of the Me 262 Project who has provided so many excellent images of their aircraft.

Thanks also to Amy at The History Press for making this happen, to my wife Ute for her support and assistance with the many German translations, and to Anna and Jay who have so many good ideas for future titles.

A number of publications and other sources were consulted in the production of this book, including: *American Raiders* by Wolfgang W.E. Samuel, *Last Talons of the Eagle* by Gary Hyland and Anton Gill, *German Aircraft of the Second World War* by J.R. Smith and Anthony Kay, *The Last Year of the Luftwaffe* by Alfred Price, *Me 262 Stormbird Rising* by Hugh Morgan, *War Prizes* by Phil Butler, *Yeager* by Chuck Yeager, *Jagdgeschwader 7 'Nowotny'* by Robert Forsyth and the *Report of the Fedden Mission in Germany*.

John Christopher, 2010

INTRODUCTION

Reichsmarshall Hermann Goering, the flamboyant and egotistical commander of Hitler's Luftwaffe, once famously boasted in 1939 that no enemy bomber could ever reach Germany's industrial heartland: 'If one reaches the Ruhr, my name is not Goering. You may call me Meyer.' It was a statement that would come back to haunt him.

The strength of the Luftwaffe lay in its ability to take the offensive in support of Germany's land forces, especially during the Blitzkrieg – the wholesale lightning invasion of its immediate neighbours. Yes, the RAF had given them a bloody nose during the Battle of Britain in the summer of 1940, but Goering's fighters still ruled the skies above occupied Europe. They continued to inflict heavy losses on both RAF Bomber Command and the United States Army Air Force (USAAF), to the extent that by the autumn of 1943 the Allies had suspended their deep-penetration raids. But that was all about to change as the tide of war turned against Germany, both on the ground and in the air. By the spring of 1944, the USAAF had introduced the P-51 Mustang, a fighter capable of escorting the bombers to their targets, and

➤ *The Messerschmitt Me 262 was the world's first operational turbojet. (Jim Larsen)*

Since the re-establishment of the German Armed Forces, Hermann Goering has been the creator of the German Air Force. It is granted to but few mortals in the course of their lives to create a military instrument from nothing and to develop it until it became the mightiest weapon of its kind.

Adolf Hitler, speaking before the Reichstag, 19 July 1940

on 6 June the Allies established a foothold on the European mainland with the D-Day landings at Normandy. For the remainder of the war, hordes of Allied bombers – literally thousands at a time – would rain destruction upon Germany's industrial centres, its oil refineries and, in a bid to undermine the morale of the civilian population and bring the war to an early close, upon its cities. In derision, the beleaguered Germans referred to the frequent wail of the air-raid sirens as 'Meyer's trumpets'.

For the stricken Reich, hope of salvation lay in a number of wonder weapons devised by its scientists and engineers. Some, such as the V-, *Vergeltungswaffe* or Vengeance weapons – the V-1 flying bomb and V-2 ballistic missile – were designed to strike fear and dread into the hearts of the enemy's cities, principally through the devastating

The Me 262 was an incredible aircraft, deservedly regarded as a legend in the annals of military aviation. The first turbojet to enter service, it was a powerful and deadly machine that was more than a match for its adversaries. The Luftwaffe pilots loved it for its speed, causing the German fighter-ace Adolf Galland to comment after his first flight that it was 'as if pushed by angels.' However, for the Allied bomber crews and their escorts it was the one thing they most feared. Faster in level flight than anything they could throw at it, the Me 262's sleek airframe, triangular in cross-section with a long tapered snout, gave it the appearance of a menacing shark. It looked right, it flew right and it went on to inspire a new generation of jet-fighter aircraft.

▲ *Me 262A-2a – formerly Yellow 7 of JG7 and now at the RAF Museum in Hendon, London.*

attacks upon London. While others, such as the rocket-powered Messerschmitt Me 163 Komet and the twin-engined jet, the Me 262, were expected to decimate the Allied raiders.

◄ *Me 262A-1c taking-off at the Luxembourg Airshow, 2008. (Jean-Marie Spapen)*

➤ *US 8th Air Force B-17 Flying Fortress during a daylight raid on the Focke-Wulf plant at Marienburg, October 1943. (US Department of Defense)*

Despite the Me 262's undoubted superiority, it was far too little and far too late to turn the fortunes of the last year of the Second World War to Germany's favour. Around 1,430 were built, and although a number were carted away as spoils of war by the victorious Allies only eight wartime Me 262s have survived, and none of these are currently airworthy. In addition there are five replicas – either completed and already flying, or still under construction – as part of the Me 262 Project based in the USA.

This is the story of the Me 262, a celebration of the world's first combat turbojet which has become universally known as the *Sturmvogel* or 'Stormbird'!

Did you know?
The Me 262 was not the only German jet operational in the Second World War. The Arado Ar 234 Blitz served as a bomber and reconnaissance aircraft, while the small Heinkel He 162 Volksjäger only entered service in the final days of the conflict.

➤ *White 35, the two-seater Me 262B-1a trainer at the DVHAA Freedom Aviation Museum at Willow Grove, Pennsylvania. (Brenden Sgalio)*

14

Although the Me 262 was regarded as the last great hope for the Luftwaffe battling to save the Reich in the final phase of the Second World War, its origins can be traced back to before the start of the war.

Credit for initiating this radical development programme lies with a small number of officials within the state air ministry, the *Reichsluftfahrtministerium* (RLM). In 1938, Hans Mauch and Helmut Schlep of the power-plant-development division within the technical group initiated an official jet-engine programme, while Hans Antz of the airframe-development department had started a complementary programme for jet and rocket-powered airframes. This was a particularly visionary concept at a time when the Luftwaffe was

Did you know?
Wilhelm Emil 'Willy' Messerschmitt was born on 26 June 1898, five and a half years before the first heavier-than-air powered flight. He died in 1978.

◄ *Front view of Tango Tango at rest during the ILA 2008, Berlin. (Jan Honcu)*

rapidly establishing its aerial supremacy through conventional piston-powered aircraft. Not surprisingly, many of the older and more conservative members among the organisation's hierarchy saw little need for such a radical step and had no enthusiasm for the project. It was almost beyond comprehension that in a few years' time the Luftwaffe would be engaged in a last desperate battle to stem an overwhelming force that would sweep across Europe and engulf the Fatherland.

Undaunted by the many detractors, Antz set his airframe-development programme into motion and succeeded in persuading Willy Messerschmitt to begin studies into a turbojet to meet the RLM's stipulations for a flight endurance of one hour at a speed of 528mph (850km/h). Chief of development at Messerschmitt was Robert Lusser, and heading up the technical team to design the new aircraft was Dr Woldemar Voigt. The initial issue was where to place the engine, or engines, and in particular the position of the intake ducts. One option was a single jet engine within the

◄ Replica of the single-engined He 178 which was the first aircraft to fly with jet power, on display in the arrival hall at Rostock-Laage Airport. (Gryffindor)

◄◄ Albert Speer, Reich Minister for Armament and War Production, on the left, with Generalfeldmarschall Erhard Milch of the Luftwaffe and Willy Messerschmitt in May 1944. (Bundesarchiv 183-H28426)

Me 262 V3 photographed at Leipheim Airfield shortly before its first flight on 18 July 1942. Note the tail-dragger wheel arrangement with the nose pointing upwards.

fuselage itself with its intake situated in the nose, but this presented potential problems concerning the centre of gravity (CoG) with an as yet undefined engine and also had the disadvantage of the jet exhaust pointing straight at the tail. (The latter was resolved in some later jets by mounting the tail higher up on a tail boom.) Under the project designation P.1065, a twin-engined layout was formulated with the engines mounted within the wings to allow flexibility in accommodating differing engines while maintaining a correct CoG.

In June 1939, three months before the start of the war, designs for P.1065 were submitted to the RLM officials and a

While through no choice of our own, the techniques involved in creating the Messerschmitt jet fighter embodied higher than usual risks, our approach to the problems was still a valid and responsible one, and the results spoke for themselves.

Woldemar Voigt, Messerschmitt engineer,
Air International, 1976

◄ Side view of an Me 262A-1a – a captured aircraft christened by Watson's Whizzers as Doris and then Jabo Bait, shown here after its arrival in the USA with FE-110 markings applied. (USAF)

wooden mock-up was completed for their inspection by March 1940. As the airframe programme was running ahead of the jet engines it was decided to reposition the engines, mounting them beneath the wings to greatly simplify the spar design. Because the intended BMW 003 turbojets were heavier than anticipated, the wings were also swept back by 18.5 degrees to properly position the CoG and thus, unintentionally, the Me 262 became the first swept-wing aircraft, although the sweep was too slight

▲ *Close-up of the Me 262's starboard-engine nacelle housing a Junkers Jumo 004.*

for any appreciable benefits in terms of speed. Initially the wing section between the fuselage and engine nacelles remained unswept, although this was later swept to the same angle as the outer wing.

Now known as the Me 262, an order was placed for three prototypes for flight testing.

These were completed by early 1941, but with no turbojets the first prototype, Me 262 V1 (PC-U1), was powered by a conventional Junkers 210G piston engine fitted in the nose space intended for the weapons. In this configuration, it commenced flight studies of the airframe and a first flight was made from Augsburg on 18 April 1941, with Fritz Wendel at the controls. By this time the rival Heinkel He 280 had already flown under jet-power with two HeS-8 turbojets – see Chapter 3, Entering the Jet Age.

An initial attempt to fly the Me 262 with two BMW 003s took place on 25 March 1942, but luckily the piston engine was still in place as the turbojets flamed-out due to compressor-blade failure shortly after take-off. The first true jet-powered flight, using the third prototype Me 262 V3 (PC-UC) fitted with Jumo 004s, took place at Leiphein Airfield on 18 July 1942. This highly successful flight lasted twelve

▼ Tango-Tango on the runway at the ILA 2008, Berlin. This is the first of the single-seater flying replicas produced by the Me 262 Project in the USA. (Jan Honcu)

minutes, with Wendel attaining an altitude of 6,560ft (2,000m) and a speed of 372mph (600km/h).

One very obvious change during the test-flight period was the move away from the 'tail-dragger' wheel configuration, which not only restricted the pilot's view during taxiing and initial take-off roll but also caused the exhaust to deflect off the runway, creating turbulence which negated the effect of the elevators. Furthermore, as the acceleration on the early jets was notoriously sluggish, the test pilots had to devise a technique of gently dabbing the brakes at take-off speed in order to raise the tail. A more permanent fix came with the fifth prototype, Me 262 V5 (PC-UE), which had a tricycle undercarriage with a fixed nose-wheel. By the time V3 was demonstrated to Hitler in November 1943 the Me 262 had a fully retractable undercarriage.

In April 1943, Generalleutnant Adolf Galland (General der Jagdflieger) flew the Me 262 V4 (PC-UD) and this influential former sceptic was immediately won over to the jet's cause. In December 1943, Hitler gave the order that full-scale production of the Me 262 should commence immediately. Controversially, he also stipulated that it should be deployed not as a defensive fighter, but as a bomber instead.

Did you know?
The Heinkel He 180 never went into production, but it was the first aircraft to feature a compressed-air ejector seat.

Even before it had entered service, the Messerschmitt 262 was in the grip of an identity crisis. Originally it had been destined to be a defensive fighter-interceptor, but after seeing a flying demonstration of the prototype Me 262 V3 at Insterburg Airfield on 26 November 1943, Hitler asked if it was capable of carrying bombs. The answer to this was yes, it could, although this begged the question of whether it should carry them. The following month he gave the order that the Me 262 should become an offensive *Schnellbomber*, a 'Fast Bomber'.

In many respects, this change of direction was not that unreasonable given that many of the Luftwaffe's conventional fighter aircraft were often equipped to carry bombs. At first, Hitler's interest was directed in using the jets to continue the bombing raids on England – which would certainly have been a waste of their capabilities – but perhaps his greater concern was to deal effectively with the long-anticipated Allied invasion of north-west Europe. The Me 262's superior speed would make it virtually invulnerable to attack by Allied aircraft, and by slowing the

▼ *Me 262A-1a, Wk/nr.11372, is the only example on display in the UK and is shown here at the RAF Museum, Hendon.*

▲ *The business end of the Me 262 showing the outlets for two of the four MK108 30mm-calibre cannon. (Jan Honcu)*

enemy's advance and containing them on the beaches it would buy him vital time in which to reposition his reserve forces to repel the invaders. The outcome of this battle would undoubtedly determine the future course of the war.

Despite the Führer's directives, Generalfeldmarschall Milch, who was responsible for the Luftwaffe's aircraft production, pushed ahead with the fighter version, the Me 262A-1a. This was known as the *Schwalbe* or 'Swallow' because of its high speed and the distinctive shape of its swept wings. With a wingspan of 41ft (12.6m) the *Scwalbe*'s all-metal fuselage had a rounded triangular cross-section which was designed primarily to accommodate the main retractable undercarriage in its belly. As a result, the pilot was placed in a high position with good all-round visibility. At

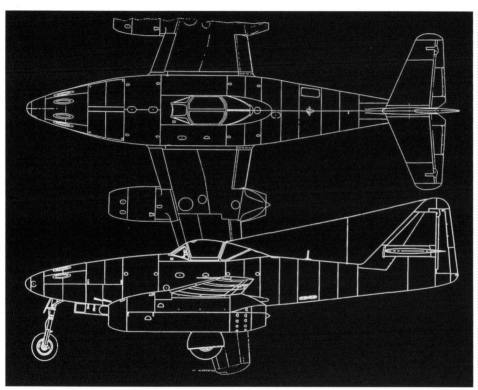

◀ *Messerschmitt plan and elevation of the Me 262A-1a Scwalbe, or Swallow.*

Did you know?
The MK108 30mm calibre Maschinenkanone, or machine cannon, built by Rheinmetall-Borsig, was a devastatingly effective weapon. On average, just four hits were enough to bring down a B-17 Super Fortress, while a single hit could down a fighter aircraft.

Did you know?

The first operational jet-fighter flown by the Allies was the British-built Gloster Meteor which entered service in July 1944, three months after the Me 262.

the rear of the aircraft was a triangular fin with a mid-height tailplane and elevators. Armaments consisted of four short-barrel MK 108 30mm cannon, housed within the nose. The fuel tanks were located fore and aft of the cockpit.

Power was supplied by two Jumo 004B turbojets generating 1,980lb (900kg) of thrust each, and in terms of performance the aerodynamically efficient Me 262A-1a could outclass any other aircraft in existence. Its maximum level speed at 23,000ft (7,000m) was a scorching 540mph (870km/h) in winter, and just slightly less in the warmer air of summer. The only possible drawback the turbojets presented, putting issues of availability and reliability aside, was with acceleration and deceleration rates in level flight, which were less than some conventional aircraft. Although the

Me 262 was incapable of breaking the sound barrier, despite unproven claims to the contrary, it came very close to it

in a dive at Mach 0.86; that's 620mph (1,000km/h). And it is worth noting that Willy Messerschmitt always regarded the Me 262 as an interim model leading to future transonic designs.

By late May 1944, thirteen pre-production fighter aircraft, designated as Me 262A-Os, had already been delivered when Hitler questioned Goering and Milch regarding progress with his *Schnellbomber*. They sheepishly informed the Führer that almost all of their efforts had been concentrated on the fighter version, and only the prototype Me 262 V10 had been modified with bomb pylons to undertake high-speed bombing tests. Hitler flew into an absolute rage upon discovering that his orders had been ignored, and when the Allies did land at Normandy only a couple of weeks later, on 6 June 1944, not one

Me 262 was there to repel the invaders. Mainly due to delays in the mass production of the engines, the first unit to receive the Me 262, the 3 Staffel (Squadron) Kampfgeschwader 51, only began training on the new aircraft on 20 June and was not operational until six weeks after D-Day.

▲ *Access hatch lifted to reveal the starboard gun bay with MK 108 30mm cannon. (DVHAA)*

▲ Cockpit interior of Me 262A-1a. (National Museum USAF)

The Me 262 was almost impossible to catch in a straight chase; its speed prevented Allied ground radar from tracking it, and the only way of bringing it down was by extremely hazardous power-dives which stressed the best Allied piston-engined fighters to the limit.

Encyclopaedia of Air Warfare, 1974

Hitler finally agreed to accept production of the fighter version, provided that it was in unison with the Me 262A-2a, the bomber variant known as the *Sturmvogel* or 'Stormbird' – a name that became widely applied to all Me 262s. By the time the Allies had established a firm foothold within Europe, production returned to the defensive fighter version on the proviso that they could be easily converted if required. The definitive version was equipped with racks to carry either a single 2,200lb (1,000kg) bomb, two 1,100lb (500kg) or two 550lb (250kg) bombs, plus standard armaments. The Me 262A-2a/U1 only had two of the cannon to make space for bomb-site equipment (see Chapter 6 – Me 262 Variants). On the main production model of the Me 262A-2a Stormbird, the protective armour was largely eliminated and an extra fuel tank added in order to increase range. One method of increasing the bomb and fuel capacity under consideration was the *Deichselschlepp* towed-bomb concept which entailed a 2,200lb (1,000kg) winged bomb pulled along behind the aircraft on a 13ft (4m) tow bar and jettisoned on target. Initial tests were carried out with the prototype Me 262 V10, but the results did not merit further development.

Could the Stormbird have turned the course of the war if it had been ready in time for D-Day? It is a purely hypothetical scenario of course, as the delays in production, in particular with the turbojets, meant that the Me 262 was far too little too late.

◀ *Me 262A-1a at the RAF Museum in Hendon.*

Did you know?

Flight testing of the prototype Me 262 V1 commenced in April 1941, although initially it was fitted with a conventional piston engine driving a propeller in the nose as the jet engines were not ready.

During the Second World War, German scientists and engineers were at the forefront of an astonishing array of aviation technologies including the first rocket-powered and turbojet aircraft, the first ballistic missile and the first pulsejet-powered aircraft and flying bombs.

The birth of the German turbojets can be traced back to the early 1930s, when Hans von Ohain began researching the subject at the University of Göttingen. While von Ohain was aware of the work of another pioneer, Frank Whittle in Britain, he did not have comprehensive information on Whittle's designs and is generally credited with producing his engines in parallel. By 1935 von Ohain was able to demonstrate the principle of his turbojet, and the following year he attracted the interest of the Heinkel company for whom he produced the HeS-1

which featured a centrifugal compressor, annular combustion chamber and radial inflow turbine, and was fuelled by hydrogen. Producing a static thrust of around 551lb (250kg), this engine was successfully bench-tested in 1937 and led directly to the development of the first turbojet flight engine, the HeS-3. This was basically a tidied-up and more compact version of the HeS-1 converted to burn liquid fuel.

In the summer of 1939 an HeS-3B was mounted within the fuselage of the prototype Heinkel He 178, and the world's

Since the Me 262 had dropped the BMW units and switched to using the same Jumo engines as some of the He 280s, the combination had proved irresistible.

Gary Hyland and Anton Gill, *Last Talons of the Eagle*, 1998

first flight on turbojet power took place on 27 August. Several further designs were instigated, most notably the more powerful HeS-8 centrifugal turbojet which, with the support of the RLM, became the first production model. It was not until 1941 that the HeS-8 was ready for flight testing, and on 2 April two of the engines carried the Heinkel He 280 prototype on its maiden flight. This aircraft was intended as a rival design to the Me 262, but by this time Heinkel were up against some serious competition.

When the RLM had launched its turbojet-development programme in 1938 (see Chapter 1 – Birth of a Legend) it was BMW and Junkers Motoren (Jumo) who were awarded contracts the following year for the development of a turbojet producing a static thrust of 1,496lb (680kg), even though Heinkel were already working on the von Ohain engines. BMW's initial efforts were concentrated on a counter-rotating axial-flow design, but this was later abandoned in favour of an axial-flow engine and this became the BMW 109-003, or 003 as it is known, which first ran

▼ *Me 262A-1a on display with an example of the Junkers Jumo 004 turbojet at the National Museum of the USAF. (Jim Kershner)*

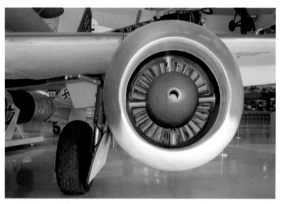

▲ Front-on view of a Jumo 004 jet-engine nacelle.

▲▶ The He 178 was the world's first jet aircraft to fly when it took off on 27 August 1939. It was powered by a single Heinkel HeS-3 jet engine designed by Hans von Ohain. (USAF)

in August 1940. Its output was a meagre 331lb (150kg) however, and when the prototype Me 262 V1 attempted to fly with two of these engines, in November 1941, turbine failures occurred on both engines shortly after take-off. It would take BMW a further two years to raise the output of their engines to 1,760lb (800kg), and by the time the 003 entered production in 1944 it had been ear-marked by the RLM for the Heinkel He 162, and not the Me 262.

In the event, it was BMW's rival, Junkers, who produced the Jumo 004 engine that would power the Me 262. Under the guidance of Dr Anselm Franz, this design utilised an axial compressor which allowed a continuous straight flow through

the engine. It also had a smaller cross-section which is essential for high-speed aircraft and, just as with the design of the Me 262 itself, Junkers put the emphasis on

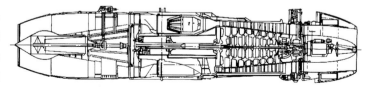

33

the simplicity of production. The engine ran on three types of fuel – J-2 a synthetic fuel produced from coal, diesel oil, or aviation gasoline – although the latter was not ideal because of its very high rate of consumption.

The first of the Jumo turbojets, the 109-004A, began bench-runs by November 1940, although it was not until 15 March 1942 that it was ready to be test-flown beneath a Messerschmitt Bf 110. They were subsequently fitted to the prototype Me 262 V3 (PU-UC) for the aircraft's first true jet flight on 18 July 1942. The RLM immediately placed an order for eighty engines, and by October that year the

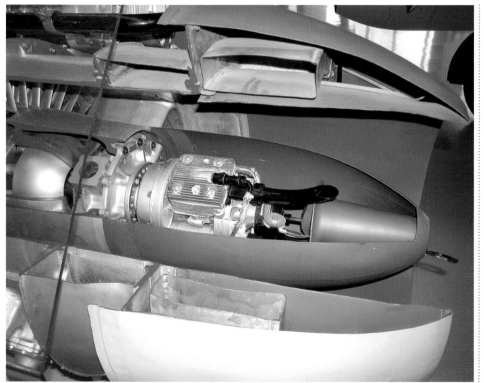

◄ *Front of the Jumo 004, with cutaway revealing the starter engine, a 10hp Riedel two-stroke engine, concealed within the intake cone. The starter handle can be seen protruding on the right.*

The exhaust of the Jumo 004 featured a variable geometry nozzle, nicknamed the Zwiebel or onion, which could be moved forward and aft to alter the exhaust area to control thrust.

▼ *This Jumo 004-engined Arado 234B reconnaissance/bomber displayed at the NASM is fitted with RATO rockets to assist with take-off. (Kogo)*

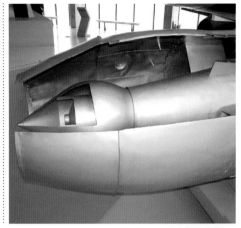

design of the production version, the 109-004B, was completed. The first of these were delivered early the following year and successfully test-flown on Me 262 V1 on 2 March 1943. A series of engine vibration problems held up full production until early 1944, and this seriously delayed the introduction of the Me 262 into service.

One drawback with the early turbojets was their short service life; in the case of the Jumo 004B some ten to twenty-five hours, although it is said that a skilled pilot could stretch this to almost double. The 004B was also sluggish in acceleration and deceleration, and pilots had to be careful not to throttle up too quickly. In addition, the starter system proved troublesome at times. This consisted of a Riedel 10hp two-stroke engine located within the air-intake cone, with a small starter pull-handle accessed through its nose and the gasoline tanks fitted in the annular intake.

Approximately 8,000 Jumo 004s were manufactured during the war. In addition to powering the Me 262, they were fitted to the twin-engined Arado 234 reconnaissance-bomber and to the prototypes of the Horton Ho 229, while the single-engined He 162 Volksjäger fighter was powered by the BMW 109-003. An improved version of the Jumo engine, the 004D, was ready to enter production and replace the 004B at the time of Germany's surrender in May 1945.

▲ The wooden framed He 162 Volksjäger was powered by a single BMW 003 turbojet. Supposedly simple to build and to fly, it was the fastest of the German jets.

When the Me 262 first engaged with the aircraft of the US Eighth Air Force in the summer of 1944, the Americans were stunned by its appearance. Not just because of its outstanding speed but, more significantly, because no one had been expecting such advanced technology to emerge from the ruins of a war-torn Reich. One of the most remarkable aspects of this story of Germany's Second World War jets is that the first, the He 178, had flown in August 1939, before German troops had marched into Poland, and yet the Allies knew nothing about them.

The world's first operational jet squadron, Erprobungskommando 262, or Ekdo 262, was formed in December 1944. Based at Lager-Lechfeld in Bavaria, the squadron was equipped with the Me 262A-1a as an experimental proving detachment and to train a core of pilots on the new aircraft. On 25 July 1944 the unit claimed its first victory when Leutnant Alfred Schreiber damaged an RAF Mosquito reconnaissance aircraft which subsequently crashed on landing. The first Me 262 lost in combat was shot down near Brussels by a pair of P-47 Thunderbolts on 28 August 1944. Following the death of the unit's

The distinctive swept wings of the Me 262A-1a Schwalbe are clearly seen in this shot of the Tango-Tango replica flying at the Luxembourg Airshow in Bitburg, Germany, June 2008. (Jean-Marie Spapen)

commander, Werner Thierfelder, in July 1944, Major Walter Nowotny was assigned as commander and the unit was later re-designated as Kommando Nowotny. Sorties against the USAAF bomber formations were instigated in August 1944, and it is claimed that the jets downed nineteen Allied aircraft for the loss of six Me 262s. On 8 November 1944 Nowotny was himself killed in action when his and two other Me 262s were shot down by American fighter escorts.

▲ White wolf emblem of the Jagdgeschwader 7 'Nowotny'.

◄ Wartime image of an Me 262A-1a. (Messerschmitt)

➤ *Luftwaffe ace Adolf Galland was an enthusiastic supporter of the Me 262 and in January 1945 he took command of the elite JG7 fighter unit. (Bundesarchiv 146-2006-0123)*

Did you know?

The largest number of daytime-fighter sorties by Me 262s on a single day was fifty-seven, carried out on 7 April 1945. Even at their peak of activity, less than 200 of the jets were serving with combat units.

In January 1945, Jagdeschwader 7, or JG7, had been formed as a pure fighter unit and the following month it was joined by Jagdverband 44, JV 44, under the command of the celebrated ace Lieutenant General Adolf Galland who had been dismissed as Inspector of Fighters by this time. Drawing upon the most experienced fighter pilots available from other units, many grounded by lack of fuel, Galland created an elite unit at a time when trained pilots were in increasingly short supply. Meanwhile, the 1 Gruppe Kampfgeschwader 54, KG 54, was created as the first of several fighter-bomber units equipped with the Me 262A-2a to undertake ground attacks. In addition, several radar-equipped Me 262B-1a/U1 night fighters entered service with 10 Staffel, Nachtjagdgeschwader II in defence of Berlin (Chapter 5 – Nahctjäger – Night Fighter.)

Large-scale attacks against the enemy bombers took place from March 1945 onwards, and on 18 March, thirty-seven Me 262s of Jagdeschwader JG7 intercepted a force of over 1,200 bombers and its accompanying swarm of 632 escort fighters. Twelve bombers and one fighter were destroyed at the cost of three

▼ *Reproduction of the R4A rack holding twelve air-to-air rockets mounted beneath the wing of an Me 262. In this case, the Yellow 5 static-display aircraft. (Me 262 Project)*

> We need the Me 262 above all else, above U-boats, and above tanks, because without these aircraft any kind of armaments production will be impossible.
>
> Field-Marshall Milch, joint conference between German Air and Munitions Ministries, January 1944

Me 262s; although an acceptable ratio in operational terms for the Luftwaffe perhaps, it represented an almost negligible loss for the raiders.

This new era of the jet brought with it a whole new approach to tactics, both for the Luftwaffe pilots and for the bomber crews and their fighter escorts. The standard procedure for the German jets was to approach the bomber formations from the rear at higher altitude, then to scream downwards past them to gain speed and then climb back to their level and open fire at a range of 1,970ft (600m). The bomber's gunners found that their electric gun turrets could not keep pace with the jets and they had no time for target acquisition. However, the Me 262's rapid closure rate upon a slow bomber also meant that the German pilots had to react very quickly as

they could easily overshoot their targets. Around sixty Me 262s were equipped with the new R4M unguided air-to-air missiles, first used in March 1945. Their tactic was to approach from the side, where a bomber's silhouette created the widest target, and fire a salvo of rockets while still out of range of the bomber's guns.

▲ Although more than 1,400 Me 262s were built, it is estimated that only around 300 saw combat.

➤ A superb view of an Me 262 in flight, the Tango-Tango replica produced by the Me 262 Project. (Jim Larsen)

No one was eager to be on the receiving end of the twin-engined German jet fighters that screamed down on our formations to quickly hit and run. The jets had a 150mph speed advantage over the Mustang, but their pilots tried to avoid dogfights, concentrating instead on hammering the bombers.

Chuck Yeager, USAF pilot, Yeager, 1985

Despite the Me 262's obvious superiority in terms of level speed, the Allied fighter pilots quickly developed new tactics of their own, often flying high above the bombers and diving down on the jets in order to gain extra speed. The German jets were less manoeuvrable than a P-51 Mustang, and by this means they could catch an Me 262 in a turn. The German pilots tried to avoid dogfights and the American pilots would accuse them of 'just teasing around'.

The Me 262, however, did have its Achilles heel. It took a long time for the Jumo 004B engines to throttle up, and the rate of acceleration and deceleration was relatively slow, making them especially vulnerable to attack during take-off and landing approaches. The Allied fighters would patrol airfields identified as jet bases

in order to swoop down like hawks upon their prey. In response, the Luftwaffe assigned FW-190s to protect the air bases when fuel supplies permitted.

▲ Fast and highly durable, the North American Aviation Mustang was a long-range fighter used extensively as a bomber escort. (National Museum USAF)

Up Against the German Jets

NORTH AMERICAN P-51 MUSTANG

From the spring of 1944, the USAAF was able to provide long-range protection for its bomber formations with the P-51 Mustang fighter which was capable of escorting them all the way to Berlin. The Mustangs were generally 50mph (80km/h) faster than their main Luftwaffe adversary, the Focke-Wulf Fw 190, and consistently out-paced them in a dive, although there was little to choose between them in a climb. But with a maximum speed of 437mph (703km/h) they were still about 130mph (200km/h) slower than an Me 262A-1a. Armed with six 0.5-inch (12.7mm) Browning machine guns, the P-51D became the primary escort fighter in the European theatre.

LOCKHEED P-38 LIGHTNING

The distinctive twin-boom and twin-engined P-38 Lightning had the range to escort bombers, but was not available in the same numbers as the P-51D. Maximum speed was 440mph (712km/h), and it was armed with one 20mm cannon and four 12.7mm Brownings.

REPUBLIC P-47 THUNDERBOLT

The chunky stalwart of the USAAF, the P-47 thunderbolt was effective in air combat and was also suited to ground attacks with its eight 12.7mm machine guns. Maximum speed was 430mph (695km/h).

As the war progressed, the Allied strategic bombing of Germany's major cities gathered pace. For Berlin, these raids varied from all-out attacks, such as the one on the night of 23 August 1943 by 727 RAF Lancaster, Halifax and Short Stirling heavy-bombers – part of 'Bomber' Harris's so-called 'Battle of Berlin' – to on-going hit-and-run raids by small groups of fast and highly manoeuvrable Mosquitos. By the latter stages of the war, the Mosquitos had been bombing the German capital with such regularity that their raids became become known as 'The Berlin Express' by the British. Despite Goering's assurances that the Luftwaffe would provide a protective umbrella over the Reich, the preparations for the defence of Berlin – in the form of an extensive ring of anti-aircraft flak guns, searchlights and even public air-raid shelters – had actually been in hand since 1939, which suggests that the authorities had always recognised that such raids were going to be on the cards.

For the most part, the bombers arrived over Berlin under the cover of darkness

▼ *The nose of this Me 262B-1a/U1 night-fighter, Red 8, bristles with Hirschgeweih antennae. Note the additional fuel tanks slung beneath the fuselage. (Raoul Blignaut)*

▶ Elevation drawing of the Me 262B-1a/U1 Nachtjäger.

and the intercepting German fighter aircraft were directed to them by ground radar tracking stations – a system that was known as *Zahme Sau* or 'Tame Boar'. From 1942, many of the Nachtjäger, the night-fighters, typically Ju 88Gs and BF 110G-4s, were equipped with early Lichtenstein FuG (*Funk-Gerät*) 202 airborne radar which operated on the 490MHz wavelength or low UHF band via a complicated array of antennae known as *Matratze* or 'mattress'. An improved version of this system which provided longer range, the FuG 212 C-1, was available by 1943, but by then the British had temporarily rendered the German radar virtually useless by dropping thousands of strips of tin foil called 'Window' (nowadays known as chaff). To counter this blocking by Window and other electronic means, Luftwaffe Major Hajo Herrmann proposed

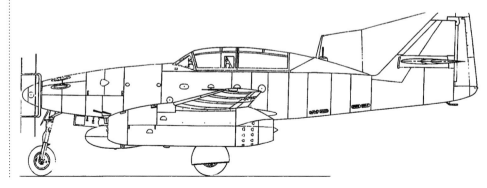

◄ *Me 262 V056 served as a test aircraft for Messerschmitt and is shown here with night-fighter antennae. The open panels provide access to the MK 108 cannon.*

For the first time I was flying by jet propulsion! No torque and no lashing sound of the engine propeller... It was as though angels were pushing.

Adolf Galland, Luftwaffe pilot and General der Jagdfieger 1941-1945

the *Wilde Sau* or 'wild boar' tactic, in which the fighters would loiter at height in order to visually locate the bombers against the glare of target indicator flares, searchlights or the burning buildings beneath them. By late 1943, the greatly improved FuG 220 SN-2, operating on a longer 90MHz wavelength, became operational and this was far less prone to electronic jamming. In this constant game of technological catch-up, the RAF aircraft soon had a new device, 'Serrate', which could actually home in on the Lichtenstein SN-2 emissions to enable them to turn the tables to hunt the German hunters.

With its superior speed, the Me 262 was an obvious candidate to deal with the marauding Mosquitos, and in September 1944 trials were conducted at the Erprobungsstelle (test station) at Rechlin

Did you know?
There is no evidence that the Me 262 ever exceeded Mach 0.86 in a dive, but it should be noted that the speed of sound, Mach 1, is not constant. It varies depending on air density.

using an Me 262A-1a fitted with SN-2 radar. Encouraged by the results, a handful of Me 262B-1a twin-seater trainers were upgraded as interim Me 262B-1a/U1 night-fighters with on-board FuG 218 Neptun radar and the distinctive *Hirschgeweih* 'stag's antler' antenna bristling from their snouts. One unfortunate effect of this type of antennae, however, was that the increased drag cut the aircraft's speed by as much as 37mph (60km/h), and it was speed that gave the Me 262 its advantage in the first place.

The first experimental Nachtjäger unit, known as Kommando Stamp (later renamed Kommando Welter), was established with the task of defending Berlin. On the night of 30 March 1945, Kurt Welter's aircraft shot down four Mosquitos; arguably the most accomplished of the night-fighter pilots he held the record with a tally of sixty-three kills, twenty of which were with the Me 262. In April 1945, this Me 262 unit became the 10 Staffel NJG 11, Nachtjagdgeschwader 11 – the first ever jet night-fighter squadron. However, worsening fuel shortages restricted their operations more and more and in the final weeks of the conflict the Mosquitos would wait to attack the jets as they landed. When the airfields became increasingly vulnerable to bombing raids, the Me 262s began operating from the Autobahn instead. Me 262B-1a/U1, Red 8 (Wk.nr.110305) flew operationally with 10 Staffel NJG 11 and is now on display at the South Africa War Museum in Johannesburg (see Chapter 11 – Me 262 Survivors).

In January 1945, work had commenced on a new type of Me 262 night-fighter which would carry FuG 218 and FuG 350 intercept radars with a rotating Nexos aerial – to detect British radar transmissions – within the cockpit. Only one prototype flew before the end of the war, the Me 262B-2a, which featured an extended fuselage to accommodate additional fuel tanks and two MK 108s firing obliquely upwards from behind the cockpit. Future models would have incorporated the uprated HeS-011 turbojets, a centimetric radar within the fuselage nose and further refinements including auxiliary fuel tanks mounted beneath the wings, changeable nose sections for a variety of armament combinations and vertically swivelling weapons located beside the cockpit.

◀ *Red 8 Nachtjäger shortly after being captured. (US National Archives)*

The Messerschmitt Me 262's design lent itself to a wide range of roles. However, to some extent its operational effectiveness became diffused over a growing array of variants which were produced in addition to the two main types, the Me 262 A-1a *Schwalbe* and A-2a *Sturmvogel*. There were many models produced, either as experimental prototypes or as proposed versions which never made it off the drawing board, and the result was a proliferation of variants:

Me 262 V

The V1 to V10 were prototype test models for the Me 262. V1 first flew on 18 April 1941, powered by a conventional Junkers 201G 2,100hp piston engine driving a nose-mounted propeller and then with BMW 003 turbojets in November 1941, although the turbines failed shortly after take-off. The Me 262 V3 was the first to fly with two Jumo 004A-0 pre-production engines on 18 July 1942.

Me 262A-0

Pre-production aircraft fitted with Jumo 004B turbojets.

Me 262A-1A *SCHWALBE*

Initial production version and by far the most common type built in both fighter and fighter/bomber versions. Equipped with four short-barrelled MK108 30mm cannon in the nose, it was the basis of many of the prototypes and variants.

Me 262A-1A/U1

These differed from the standard A-1a, being fitted with six nose-mounted guns;

► *Bearing the emblem and colours of JG7, the Yellow 5 static-display replica. (Me 262 Project)*

54

the upper pair of 30mm MK108s fitted to provide space for TSA bomb-sight apparatus.

Me 262A-2A/U2

Prototype of the *Loftebomber* with extended glazed nose section to accommodate a prone bomb-aimer operating a Lofte 7D level-bombing sight.

Unless the ground troops occupy Germany before June, the German production of jet and rocket fighters will make it impossible for formations of 1,000 bombers escorted by 800 fighters to continue operations.

Message from General Anderson to Eisenhower, February 1945

Me 262A-3A

Proposed ground-attack version with four MK108s, rockets and extra armour.

Me 262A-4A

An unarmed reconnaissance aircraft, abandoned in favour of the Me 262A-1a/U3.

Me 262A-5A

Definitive reconnaissance version, with two MK108 30mm cannon and equipped with two 500-litre drop tanks.

Me 262B-1A

Two-seater dual-control trainer introduced in 1944. The only surviving example is housed at the Harold F. Pitcairn Wings of Freedom Museum at NAS Willow Grove, Pennsylvannia.

Me 262B-1A/U1

Two-seat trainers converted into night-fighters with FuG 218 Neptun long-wavelength radar. Red 8 is on display at the South African National Museum of Military History in Johannesburg.

◄ *Me 262A-1a.*

▼ *The Pulkzerstörer Me 262A-1/U4 tank-buster equipped with a MK214A 50mm cannon.*

◄ Inside the double cockpit of the Me 262B-1a, White 35, twin-seater trainer which is now on display at the Delaware Valley Historical Aircraft Association Museum at Willow Grove, Pennsylvania. (DVHAA)

► Front console on pilot's left side: Throttles, fuel lever (red), and indicators and controls for tailplane trim, with landing flap and undercarriage switches and indicators at the front. (DVHAA)

◄ Front cockpit with view of main control panel. On the left-hand side are the six main flying instruments with airspeed indicator, turn and bank indicator, and variometer (rate of climb) running across the top row. Beneath them are the altimeter, direction indicator, and AFN-2 indicator. Hidden by the joystick are weapon control lights and ammo counter, and the space on the far left is for oxygen and pressure gauges. On the right-hand side are gauges for the engines with RPM indicator at the top, then fuel pressure, fuel temp, fuel injection temp, oil pressure and fuel contents. (DVHAA)

►► The Me 262 was not equipped with an ejector seat. (DVHAA)

► Front console on pilot's right: Main switchboard at the front, signal flare control box, starter control switches, FuG controls and connectors for pilot's helmet leads. (DVHAA)

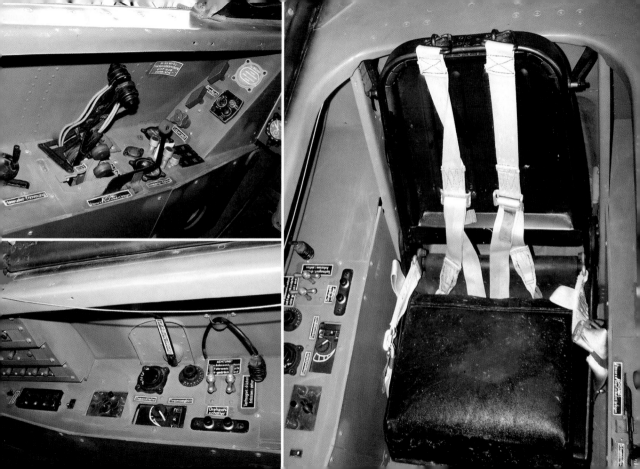

Lady Jess IV *was the name given by Watson's Whizzers to this Me 262A-1a/U3 photo-reconnaissance variant photographed at Melun in June 1945. (USAF)*

Me 262B-2A

Proposed stretched night-fighter with longer fuselage and increased fuel capacity, and two extra MK108s firing upwards from behind the cockpit.

Me 262C

Prototypes of rocket-boosted interceptor known as *Heimatschützer*. Me 262 C-1a was adapted from Me 262A Wk.nr 130186 with the addition of a Walter HWK 109-509A-2 rocket fitted in the tail. It was first flown with combined rocket/jet power on 27 February 1945. The three-minute burst of rocket thrust was enough to reduce the take-off run by at least 650ft (200m) and propelled the aircraft to 26,000ft (7,925m). The Me 262 C-2b, *Heimatschützer II*, was adapted from Wk.nr.170074 with two BMW 003R combined powerplants

comprising a BMW 003 turbojet and BMW 718 rocket mounted atop the rear of each jet. Flown only once on 26 March 1945. Me 262 C-3a was never completed.

▼ *White 1, a flying replica twin-seater designated as an Me 262B-1c by the Me 262 Project. (Andreas Mowinckel)*

Did you know?
With fuel supplies running desperately short in the latter stages of the war, a directive was issued to Luftwaffe units ordering them to have aircraft pulled into position by oxen rather than waste aircraft fuel taxiing.

Me 262D-1

Proposed interceptor variant equipped with *Jagdfaust* 50mm-upward-facing anti-bomber mortars. These had been developed for the fast Me 163s and were triggered by the shadow of a bomber falling on a photocell.

Me 262E

Proposed variant to carry up to forty-eight R4M rockets.

Several other variants were considered but mostly never built, such as the Me 262HG or *Hochgeschwindigkeit* series of high-speed interceptors capable of transonic level flight. The HG I was modified with a low-profile *Rennkabine* or racing cabin and is said to have attained 624mph (1,004km/h) in tests. The proposed HG II was to feature a thirty-five-degree swept wing and butterfly tail and designs for the HG III were more radical still, with turbojets inset into the wings.

Given that the Me 262's long snout tended to result in poor downward visibility for bomb-aiming, reconnaissance and bomber versions were conceived with the cockpit moved forward. Ramjets and pulse-jets were also under consideration, as well as a *Mistel* or 'Mistletoe' variant in which two Me 262s were mounted one above the other, with the piloted craft releasing the unmanned lower flying bomb on to its target.

When Adolf Hitler gave the order for the full-scale production of the Me 262 in December 1943, Germany's industrial heart was already being pounded by the Allied bombers. Aircraft production had been repeatedly targeted, including Messerschmitt's facilities at Augsburg and Regensburg. Wartime-aircraft output actually increased overall despite the bombings, and by January 1945 over 600 Me 262s had been delivered to the Luftwaffe. By the beginning of April this

◄ FE-1101, Me 262A-1a, during post-war appraisals in the USA. (USAF)

➤ *A scene of devastation after a bombing raid on the Me 262 manufacturing facility at Obertraubling. (US National Archives)*

▲ *A concealed underground Me 262 production facility in the Thüringen area, photographed in early 1945. (Bundesarchiv 141-2738)*

number had risen to around 1,200 through the rationalisation of production as well as measures to disperse and hide the production centres, in effect sending them underground.

For the Messerschmitt company, the large areas of forest close to its plants offered an obvious means of concealment and dispersal via a number of 'forest factories'. Consisting of low wooden buildings, these facilities took advantage of the natural cover offered by the trees which was augmented with camouflage paint or netting to very effectively avoid detection by Allied aircraft. Small enough to remain hidden, they permitted the continued production of the subsystems and

Wing detail showing ailerons.

and such widely spread buildings were too small to be individually targeted.

The company's technical department, complete with a staff of 2,000 with responsibility for the building of experimental prototypes, was transferred to Oberammergau at the end of 1943, and it was there that the Allies would discover the prototype of the single-engined P.1101 fighter at the end of the war.

In 1944, work began on a series of semi-subterranean bomb-proof bunkers in the Landsberg area, near Kaufering in Bavaria, specifically for the large-scale production of the Me 262. These were part of project *Ringeltaube*, or 'Wood Pigeon', instigated by Albert Speer's Reichsministerium für Rüstung und Kriegsproduktion (RfRuK), the Reich Ministry for Armament and War Production. Three vast cavernous arch-

assemblies, with the Autobahn serving as a makeshift runway for completed aircraft. It should be remembered that, in general, the concept of precision bombing during the Second World War meant striking the approximate vicinity of any given location,

shaped bunkers, each 1,300ft- (400m) long and 278ft- (85m) wide were to be constructed at the site, and in 1944 work commenced on the first, code-named *Weingut II*, or 'Vineyard II'.

It was constructed by heaping up tons of excavated gravel to create a former for the vast semi-cylindrical concrete roof which consisted of eight inches (20cm) of light cement interlaced with iron rods, capped with a further covering of heavy concrete. This was considered adequate to resist RAF's six-ton bombs. Once the concrete had set, the gravel was then removed and used in the construction of other parts of the structure. *Weingut II* was so vast that the plans included an underground runway for the departure of the finished Me 262s, although assistance from liquid-fuelled RATO (Rocket-Assisted

Take-Off) units would probably have been essential.

Responsibility for construction lay with the Organisation Todt, while the SS managed an army of 10,000 slave workers made up of Russian prisoners plus thousands of Jewish inmates brought from concentration camps, such as Dachau.

▲ *A line up of newly finished Me 262 outside a concealed forest factory near Obertraubling. (US National Archives)*

➤ *Undercarriage detail, starboard side, of an Me 262A-1a.*

Working fourteen-hour shifts seven days a week, conditions for the workers were appalling; their average life expectancy measured in weeks. *Weingut II* had not been completed when it was occupied by American troops in April 1945, although it is known that forced labourers from concentration camps did produce fuselages for the Me 262 elsewhere.

Landsberg was one of countless dispersed facilities, and many others were established in natural and man-made caves. Even the Autobahn tunnel at Engelberg, west of Stuttgart, was used for the production of the Me 262 wings. Likewise, the aero-engine companies sought safety underground and the Junkers engine division established a production line for the Jumo 004 within the miles of tunnels at Nordhausen in the Harz Mountains. Workers came from the nearby concentration camp known as Dora. In terms of construction, conditions in some of these far-flung facilities were

Did you know?
Although the maximum speed of the Gloster Meteor F MkI was 410mph (660 km/h), it was no match for the Me 262 which could achieve a level speed of 560mph (900km/h).

far from ideal, and in many cases the damp soon spoilt the equipment. Furthermore, a proportion of the workforce actively sought to sabotage the aircraft regardless of the terrible penalties if caught. This would range from pieces of metal swarf left in electrical junction boxes, sand in the oil systems or simply bolts and other fixings left loose. After the war, Willy Messerschmitt was sentenced to two years' imprisonment for his involvement in the use of slave labour and RfRuK Minister Albert Speer was sentenced to twenty.

In addition to protecting the production facilities, Messerschmitt and Junkers both faced shortages of materials, although this was mitigated to some extent by the airframe's simple design and extensive use of steel. As for the Jumo 004B engines, the use of materials such as nickel and cobolt was minimised and new methods of heat-proofing were developed, including aluminium coating to protect the steel fan blades against oxidisation.

The Allied bombers may have failed to bring an immediate halt to armaments production, but the raids on the rail networks, the oil fields and synthetic oil plants meant that the German war machine was slowly grinding to a halt. It is estimated that it took over 9,000 man hours to produce each Me 262 airframe and, faced with the overwhelming industrial capacity of the Allies, in particular the Americans, time was running out for the Nazi regime.

By late 1944, the Luftwaffe was facing such overwhelming odds that even the technological superiority of aircraft such as the Me 262, Me 163B and the Arado 234B could not prevent it being swamped by the sheer pressure of enemy-fighter numbers. To demonstrate that it was far from being a spent force, the Luftwaffe launched Operation *Bodenplatte*, or 'Baseplate', on New Year's Day 1945 in a bid to regain air superiority with an all-out pre-emptive attack against seventeen Allied airfields in Holland and Belgium. A force of over 1,000 aircraft was mustered for the early morning

◄ *A rocket-powered Me 163 is suspended above Hans-Guido Mutke's Me 262A-1b at the Deutsche Museum, Munich. (Danner Glyde)*

➤ *This Me 262A-2a on display at the Australian War Memorial, Canberra, is of particular interest as it is largely in original condition and gives an indication of the quality of the factory finish. (Mark Smith)*

a high price with 280 German aircraft lost, and this would be their last great single air offensive of the war.

The main reason for the operation's failure had been the poor quality of flying, especially in the accuracy of strafing runs, by a high proportion of inexperienced and poorly trained pilots. The loss of so many skilled aircrew during the long drawn-out defence of the Reich had severely curtailed the training programmes, and in the rush to fill the empty cockpits the newer pilots were often learning how to fight on the front line. It is said that the Luftwaffe had grown into two air forces; the few great aces and the mass of other pilots who had as much difficulty in landing their aircraft as they did surviving in combat. In most cases, the new pilots had been reassigned from other units and were woefully under-

raids, and as a result around 500 Allied aircraft were destroyed on the ground and many of the airfields were put out of action for some time. However, the Luftwaffe paid

trained to fly these high-performance jets which took them to the limit of their abilities and resulted in a high attrition rate.

By the end of the month around 600 Me 262s had been delivered, and of these about sixty were operational with fighter-bomber, night-fighter or reconnaissance units, a further 150 were active with the fighter units and of the remainder, around 150 had been destroyed by enemy action.

Did you know?
The Luftwaffe's night-fighters were blinded by the use of 'Window' – small strips of metal foil released by the Allied Pathfinder aircraft over their targets to confuse the German radar signals.

◀ *B-17 Flying Fortresses in formation on a bombing run to Neumunster in April 1945. (USAF)*

73

raids, large numbers of the Luftwaffe's conventional aircraft were grounded. But, even as Germany's territory contracted, the Me 262 units continued to aggressively attack the raiders, and in the right hands they took their toll on the bombers. On 14 January a force of 189 aircraft, including half a dozen Me 262s, was scrambled to intercept a wave of 900 USAAF bombers and its escorts. The Allies lost seventeen bombers and eleven of the fighter escorts, while the Germans lost 140 of theirs.

▲ Using the Autobahns as impromptu airstrips, many abandoned Me 262s were found concealed in the woods. Unusually, this example appears to be intact.

Countless others were delayed in transit on the damaged railway system. With fuel stocks dwindling and supplies from the refineries and synthetic processing plants severely hampered by the intense Allied

By March 1945 units such as Galland's Jagdverband 44 were delivering large-scale attacks, and on 18 March thirty-seven Me 262s engaged a force of over 1,200 heavy-bombers heading for Berlin. Using the R4M rockets for the first time, it is claimed that between eight and twelve of the bombers were destroyed along with one of the escort fighters. Over the following two days ten more kills were claimed, with the

Series production of jet engines in large quantities was undoubtedly in a more advanced state in Germany than in Britain and the USA, and had the war continued and had the factories not been over-run, they would have been producing several thousand jet engines per month by this autumn.

Report to the Fedden Mission to Germany, Ministry of Aircraft Production, June 1945

loss of six of the jets. By the beginning of April 1945 the British and American troops had crossed the Rhine, and on the Eastern Front the Soviets were within fifty miles of Berlin itself. This month was to be the high point of Me 262 defensive operations as the fighter sorties continued with the largest number on a single day, fifty-seven, on 7 April alone.

▲ The Me 328 was conceived as a parasite aircraft either towed or carried piggy-back, but Messerschmitt engineers considered fitting it with a Jumo 004 to create a suicide bomber. (Messerschmitt)

As April drew to its close the Luftwaffe was in tatters. Only three months earlier General Eisenhower had warned that if Hitler could have prolonged the war beyond the summer of 1945, he would have 'jets of such superior performance and in such numbers as to challenge our aerial supremacy over not only Germany but all of Western Europe'. In truth, the seeds of the Luftwaffe's destruction had been sown in the opening months of the war when its conventional piston-engined aircraft had so comprehensively gained the skies above mainland Europe to such an extent that the RLM had been blinded to the need for an effective defensive air force. If the Me 262 programme had been given priority at an earlier stage then the course of the war might have been different. As it was, this magnificent aircraft could not turn the tide of the war.

Hitler took his own life on 30 April 1945, and on 8 May Germany surrendered unconditionally.

◀ *Jumbo 004 jet engines abandoned at a forest factory near Obertrauling. (US National Archives)*

In the spring of 1945, the Allies implemented a grand supermarket sweep in order to scoop up all manner of Nazi technology and expertise which had been left behind by the retreating German forces. The purpose of this was twofold, for the Americans in particular there might be lessons to be learned which could aid their forces still fighting the Japanese, who, as Germany's former ally, had been privy to many of their latest technological innovations. In addition, the Americans, the Soviets and, to a lesser extent, the British, wanted the German hardware and scientists to aid in their fight during the peace that was soon to come. Much of the technology that bolstered the Cold War political posturing was directly descended from German wartime technology, particularly in the field of rocket research with its implications for the rise of the Intercontinental Ballistic Missile (ICBM). And, without a doubt, both sides, East and West, were in a race to grab the best of the German jet-powered aircraft.

Leading the American Air Technical Intelligence effort was Colonel 'Hal'

▼ *The nose of an Me 262A-2a looms out of the darkness at the Australian War Memorial, Canberra. (Steve Madsen)*

Watson, who was equipped with a list of target aircraft which he divided between two teams. One searched for conventional aircraft, while the other went after the jets. Intelligence reports indicated that these were to be found at Lager-Lechfeld, to the south of Augsburg in Bavaria, and this was in fact the main airfield used by Messerschmitt. Watson immediately assigned Lieutenant Robert C. Strobell to head down to Lechfeld in order to get the jets into an airworthy condition, teach the US pilots and the mechanics how to fly and maintain them, and then prepare for their shipment back to the States.

Arriving at Lechfeld at the end of May 1945, Strobell discovered that the airfield and most of its precious jets had been

◄ Wilma Jeanne – *a Pulkzerstörer Me 262 A-1/U4 tank-buster with its 50mm cannon. (USAF)*

▲ *Donald Duck rides a jet engine in the unofficial emblem for Watson's Whizzers.*

badly damaged; the former by aerial bombardment and the latter, intentionally, by the retreating Germans in a bid to keep their technology out of enemy hands. American soldiers from the 54th Disarmament Squadron had arrived a few weeks earlier and they had safeguarded as many aircraft as possible and gathered

The next thing I noticed was the speed. Raw speed, exhilarating speed. Smooth speed. Unbelievable speed. It seemed effortless. My flight was held at low altitude, so I had the ground as a reference. This was something I had never experienced in the P-47 Thunderbolt, and it was impressive.

Lieutenant Robert C. Strobell, USAF, on his first solo flight in the Me 262, June 1945

together many of the former Me 262 workforce. Pressed into service as civilian employees, the Germans took great pride in their jets and proved to be willing and cooperative with the Americans. Strobell's team soon came up to full strength with six USAAF pilots, ten crew chiefs plus the German nationals and former Messerschmitt test pilots Ludwig Hofmann and Karl Baur.

Of the Me 262s at Lechfeld, most had been cobbled together from various engines and other components salvaged on the site, although at least two had been surrendered and flown to the airfield. In addition, there was a factory two-seater training aircraft still in good condition. In total, ten aircraft were readied for flight, but the questioned remained concerning who was to fly them, as the Americans had no experience with

Did you know?
The rocket-powered Me163B Komet had a greater rate of climb than the Me 262, but its maximum dive speed of Mach 0.82 could be bettered by the more stable Me 262.

jets. In a ploy to deter any attempts at sabotage, Strobell asked Bauer to make the first flight, which lasted around fifteen minutes, and then he took his turn, only to find the aircraft's slow rate of acceleration during the take-off run meant he almost ran out of runway before lifting the jet off the ground. Once in the air, however, the

➤ *Me 262A-1a, recovered by Watson's Whizzers at Lager-Lechfeld and now on display at the National Museum USAF in Ohio. (USAF)*

➤➤ *Wrecked Jumo 004 engines discovered by the Allies at Magdeburg.*

American pilot soon discovered the joy of jet propulsion. 'The next thing I noticed was the speed. Raw speed, exhilarating speed. Smooth speed. Unbelievable speed. It seemed effortless...' With such an abundance of speed getting this bird back on the runway required some practise, and on the first approach he shot right past the airfield. The second approach was little better, but on the third he managed to coax the jet back on to the ground.

Once the USAAF pilots, including Watson, had been given orientation flights in the two-seater trainer, the task of ferrying the aircraft began in earnest on 10 June. The plan was to take them cross-country in two stages to Melun in France, and then on to the port of Cherbourg where the British escort carrier HMS *Reaper* had been made available for their transportation to the USA. With the two German pilots making up the numbers, the ten aircraft reached Melun without incident. Once there, the pilots selected new names for their aircraft, numbers were assigned to each machine, and America's first jet-fighter squadron acquired its unofficial title 'Watson's Whizzers'. In recognition of their

◀ Cockpit instruments and interior of an Me 262A-1a. (US Army Signal Corps)

◀◀ Me 262A-1a, Wk/nr.111711. (USAF)

propeller blades would be ceremoniously snapped off.

During their brief stay at Melun, the Americans put on a display for General Carl Spaatz. They also had time to investigate reports of additional Me 262s which had been recovered at other airfields. At Schleswig they found a two-seater trainer plus an Me 262B-1a/U1 night-fighter, and at Grove they located examples of the Arado Ar 234 twin-jet-powered bomber,

unusual status as jet jockeys, it became customary for each new pilot to have his metal USAAF badge removed and the

all of which were added to the hoard at Melun.

The next leg, to Cherbourg, was conducted between 30 June and 6 July. One of the first aircraft to depart from Melun was V083, the prototype Me 262A-1a/U4 armed with a 50mm MK214 tank-busting cannon, but when the Jumo's engine began spitting out turbine blades the aircraft was sent into a steep dive and the pilot, Hofmann, was only thrown clear at low altitude. In another incident, Lieutenant Robert J. Anspach descended through thick cloud expecting to see Cherbourg but instead found himself over water, and with fuel precariously low he make an emergency landing on the island of Jersey. On a second ferry flight, the unlucky Anspach experienced a dramatic landing at Cherbourg after the nose-wheel failed to lower.

In total, nearly forty aircraft of all types were loaded aboard the *Reaper*, each one wrapped in plastic film to protect it from the salty spray. Upon arrival at Newark, New Jersey, the jets were transferred to Freeman Field in Indiana for evaluation.

◄ *T2-4012 photo-reconnaissance Me 262A-1a/U3 was evaluated at Freeman Field before being loaned to Hughes Aircraft. Howard Hughes had it slicked up with the intention of taking part in air races. (USAF)*

Single-seater Avia S-92 at the Prague Aero Museum at Kelby, Czech Republic.

Today, in the overcrowded exhibition hall of Prague Aero Museum at Kbely in the Czech Republic, there are two remarkable aircraft on display, the last direct descendants of the Me 262. During the war the Germans had set up a number of construction plants within Czechoslovakia to make aircraft for the Luftwaffe, including components for the Me 262 and the Jumo 004B engines. With so many parts available, it was decided to continue production after the war was over under the designation Avia S-92 for the single-seat version and CS-92 for the two-seater, the equivalents of the Me 262A-1a and the Me 262B-1a. The airframes were built by Avia, the

> With all the data that we obtained from the Me 262 we were able to equip our pilots, still fighting the war against Japan, because we suspected that the Japanese would build an Me 262, as they did, although it wasn't a very good one...
>
> Colonel 'Hal' Watson, USAAF

biggest aircraft producer in Czechoslovakia, and the Jumo 004 turbojets came from the repair works at Malesice and were renamed as the M-04. Assembled at the Letnany Research Institute, the first flight of one of these Czech jets took place in September 1946 with Avia's chief test pilot, Antonin Kraus, at the controls.

Twelve Czech-built Me 262s were completed, nine S-92 and three CS-92. They served with the 5th Fighter Flight of the Czech Air Force from 1947 until 1951, after which they became training aids. Avia succeeded in attracting some interest from foreign customers at the time, notably the Yugoslavian government which considered acquiring two of the S-92s, but Avia closed down the production line before the deal went through so they could build the Soviet MiG 15 and the Yakovlev Yak 23 instead. Rumour that the Israeli Air Force had bought S-92s after the war are entirely unsubstantiated.

In Japan, Germany's wartime allies had created their own version of the Me 262,

▲ *Avia M-04 engine at the Prague Aero Musuem.*

➤ *The Japanese Nakajima Kikka was smaller than the Me 262. This prototype is equipped with RATO launch-assist rockets beneath the fuselage. (USAF)*

▼ *Captured Kikka at Patuxent River US Naval Air Base, Maryland, 1946. (US Navy)*

the Nakajima Kikka, which may have been shaped by information and hardware delivered by U-boat. In late 1944, the Japanese Naval Air Staff had instructed Nakajima to design a turbojet fighter-bomber, and the Navy Special Attacker Kikka (Orange Blossom) was, in essence, a smaller-scale mimic of the German jet. Compared with the Me 262's 40ft (12.2m) wingspan, the Kikka's was around 34ft (10.4m) and the straight wings folded to aid concealment in caves or shelters. Originally it was to be powered with two Tsu-11 engines, but these were replaced by the Ne-12 and later by the N2-20 (inspired by the BMW 003), and these generated 1,050lb (475kgp) each. The Kikka first flew on 7 August 1945 – the day before the first atomic bomb fell on Hiroshima – and was piloted by Lieutenant Commander Susumu

◀ *Me 262A-1a.*

Takaoka with a pair of RATO boosters assisting in the take-off.

Plans for the aircraft's production were well in hand, and a second prototype was completed, but had not yet flown, when the Japanese surrendered on 2 September 1945. As with the German jets, the Kikka was taken back to the USA for further examination as a war prize. It is now on display in the NASM in Washington.

The Soviets had fallen behind in their own development of the turbojet during the war years when, in March 1945, their army discovered an Me 262A-1a at the Kolberg-Bodenhagen Airfield. As a result, the Soviet design collectives were tasked with devising a single and a twin-jet fighter bomber around the Jumo 004 or the BMW 003 engines. They built their own approximate clone of the Me 262, the Sukhoi Su-9, a single-seat fighter equipped with copies of the Jumo 004 known as the Rd-10. The prototype flew on 13 November 1946 and it was one of the first Soviet aircraft to feature an ejector seat – based on the one used on the Heinkel He 162. The Su-9 was armed with one Nudelman N-37 37mm plus twin N-23 23mm cannon, and could

carry a payload of one 1,100lb (500kg) bomb or two 550lb (250kg) bombs.

In May 1947 a second version, the Su-11, took to the air, and this featured a number of aerodynamic improvements in addition to the more powerful Soviet Lyulka TR-1 turbojets, each giving a thrust of 2,870lb (1,300kgp). However, this line

Did you know?
The Messerschmitt company merged with Bölkow in 1968 and with Hamburger Flugzeugbau the following year to become Messerschmitt-Bölkow-Blohm (MBB). It is now part of European Aeronautic Defence & Space (EADS).

of development was abandoned in favour of other more promising designs and that, in truth, was the legacy of the Stormbird. While it had been the world's first turbojet to enter active service, outpacing any other aircraft flying at the time, ironically the subsequent development of more powerful turbojets made the twin-engine

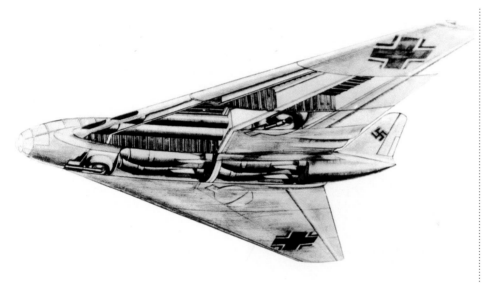

configuration obsolete. While the Me 262's influence was to be found in the swept-wing profile of the Lockheed F-80 and the North American F-86 Sabre, it was the descendants of the likes of the Messerschmitt P.1101, the single-engined interceptor, that would rule the post-war skies.

Me 262 SURVIVORS

Approximately 1,430 Me 262s were constructed during the Second World War, and of those which were left at the cessation of hostilities only a handful are known to have survived. Of the various aircraft taken away by the Allies – the majority went to the USA and the remainder to the UK, France and the USSR – there are just eight examples left in the world. The others were either destroyed in accidents or scrapped once they had outlived their usefulness. The survivors can be found in Germany, Australia, South Africa and the UK, each with one Me 262 in their various museums, and of the remaining four aircraft, three are in museums in the USA and one is owned privately. None is airworthy, currently at least, and the only flying Me 262s are the replicas which

During the final stages of World War Two the Messerschmitt 262 was the world's best, and by far most superior fighter aircraft.

Adolf Galland, *Me 262 Stormbird Rising*, 1994

are either under construction or already completed by the Me 262 Project (see Chapter 12 – The Legend Flies Again).

Me 262A-1B, WK/NR.500071 WHITE 3

On the morning of 25 April 1945, Hans-Guido Mutke found himself running short of fuel over French-occupied territory to the north of Lake Constance in southern Germany. To avoid capture, he landed his Me 262 at Zurich's Dubendorf Military Airfield in neutral Switzerland with only two minutes of fuel remaining. For the Swiss aviation industry, the first jet to land on their soil, and in such good condition, was a gift from heaven. Mutke was released

➤ *Me 262B-1a, White 35, the restored two-seater trainer at Willow Grove.*

➤➤ *Front instrument panel of the Me 262B-1a. (DVHAA)*

by the authorities six months later. Back in Germany, the Deutsches Museum pressed the Swiss to release the aircraft into their care as it was, they claimed, still German property, and in 1957 it was handed over. Today, White 3 is on display together with an Me 163 in the museum at Munich. See www.deutsches-museum.de

Me 262A-2A, WK.NR.500200 BLACK X 9K+XK

Firm details are sketchy on the operational history of this aircraft, although it is believed to have served with the 4th Staffel of II./KG 51, and been surrendered to the British at Fassberg on 7 May 1945. It arrived at Farnborough in August 1945, and was involved in performance and handling evaluations until November of that year. In 1946, it was sent as a gift to the Australian

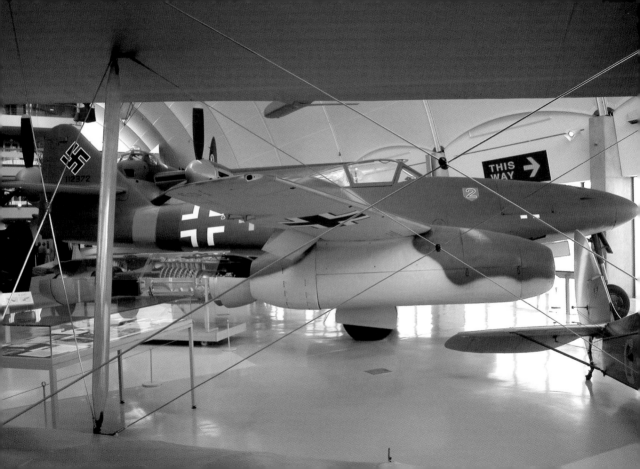

◀◀ Me 262A-2a at the RAF Museum.

◀ Red 13, formerly White 25, Me 262A-1a/U3, now owned by Paul Allen. (Jim Larsen)

Did you know?
Obsessed with speed, the American industrialist and aviation enthusiast Howard Hughes had wanted to race with an Me 262-1a/U3 in the 1947 Cleveland Air Races, but was persuaded to drop the idea.

government aboard the SS *Waipawa* and is now on display at the Australian War Memorial, Canberra. Uniquely, this aircraft has not been restored and its battered body speaks of its chequered history, including evidence of gunfire damage.

See www.awm.gov.au

Me 262B-1A/U1, WK.NR.110305 RED 8

This is the rarest of all the survivors, a two-seat night-fighter complete with its original aerials and drop tanks. It had flown with 10./NJG 11 at Magdeburg and was ferried to the UK in May 1945 to be used for radar and tactical trials, with the RAF serial number VH519. During October/November 1945 it went on public display with other German aircraft at RAE Farnborough. In early 1947, it was shipped to South Africa on board the SS *Clan McRea*

and was kept at the SAAF Central Flying School in Dunnottar until it was restored to exhibition standard in 1997. It is now on display at the South African National Museum of Military History, Johannesburg. See www.militarymuseum.co.za

Me 262A-2A, WK.NR.112372

Formerly Yellow 7 of I./JG/7 and surrendered at Fassberg, it was flown to Lubeck by Wing Commander Schrader of No.616 Squadron where it was severely damaged on landing. It was later ferried from Copenhagen to RAE Farnborough in June 1945, and made its first flight from there on 6 September 1945. The aircraft was allocated RAF serial number VK893 and flown in handling trials until 29 November 1945. Since then it has been displayed at a number of RAF stations including Cranwell, Gaydon, Finningly,

◄ *Close-up of under-wing with Luftwaffe cross emblem.*

Cosford, St Athan and is now at the RAF Museum in Hendon, London.

See www.rafmuseum.org.uk

Me 262A-1A, WK.NR.501232 YELLOW 5

Christened *Beverly Ann* and then *Screemin Meemie*, this aircraft was flown by Lt Robert Strobell, who led the retrieval of Me 262s from Lechfield to Cherbourg for the renowned Watson's Whizzers. Shipped to the USA aboard HMS *Reaper*, it was evaluated by the Flight Test Division at NAS Patuxant River until January 1946 before transfer to the Naval Aviation Supply Depot, Philidelphia. There it ended up in the airfield's dump until it was rescued in 1957 and moved to the National Museum of the US Air Force, Wright-Patterson Air Force Base, Dayton, Ohio.

See www.nationalmuseum.af.mil

Me 262A-1A, WK.NR.500491 YELLOW 7

Originally flown by Ofw. Heinz Arnold of II./JG 7, this second Yellow 7 had seven enemy kill marks adorning its fuselage when it was handed over at Lager-Lechfeld on 8 May 1945. It was allotted Watson's Whizzers' number 888 and given a string of names including *Dennis*, *Julie* and *Ginny H*. Shipped on HMS *Reaper*, it was stored at various USAF bases before being transferred to the care of the National Air & Space Museum's restoration facility at Silver Hill, Maryland, and is now on display at the Smithsonian Institution, Washington.

See www.nasm.si.edu

Me 262B-1A, WK.NR.110639 WHITE 35

A very interesting example of a single-seater which was converted to a two-seat trainer, and the only surviving example of

a relatively small number of such trainers. Captured intact at Lager-Lechfeld, White 35 was identified by Watson's Whizzers as being of particular interest and was flown via Melun to Cherbourg on 30 June 1945. 'White 35' went on display in the open air at NAS Willow Grove, Pennsylvania, until it was sent for restoration in return for acting as a pattern aircraft for the Me 262 Project. The restored two-seater now has pride of place at the Delaware Valley Historical Aircraft Association's Harold F. Pitcairn Wings of Freedom Aviation Museum, at Willow Grove.

See www.dvhaa.org

Me 262A-1A/U3, WK.NR.500453

The only privately owned Me 262 belongs to Paul Allen, the co-founder of Microsoft and a keen collector of vintage aircraft. White 25, as it was formerly known, was a photo-reconnaissance aircraft found at Lager-Lechfeld and christened by Watson's team as 'Connie – my sharp article', although later changed to 'Pick II' and given the number 444. On 19 August 1945, Colonel Watson flew it to Freeman's Field in Indiana for flight testing, and re-designated as FE-4012 it was loaned to the Hughes Aircraft Division. Restored for exhibition at the Planes of Fame collection in Chino, California, it was sold to Allen in 2000 and is currently (2009) undergoing extensive restoration in the UK, some sources say to flying condition with Jumo engines. For more on Allen's Flying Heritage Collection at Everett, Washington, please visit the website listed below.

See www.flyingheritage.com

G iven the iconic nature of the Me 262 Stormbird, it was only to be expected that hardcore aviation enthusiasts would dream of getting one flying again, and a little over half a century after the fall of the Luftwaffe at the end of the Second World War, they did just that.

The Me 262 Project owes its origins to the American industrialist Stephen L. Snyder who formed Classic Fighter Industries in the early 1990s with the goal of building a new generation of Stormbirds. With only a handful of original airframes still in existence (see Chapter 11 – Me 262 Survivors), it was determined that none were suitable for restoration to flight standards and the only option was to create replicas. From the beginning, the objective was to create an aircraft that not only looked like the original, but was faithful to its spirit in every detail.

To accomplish this they needed to get their hands on an existing Me 262 as a template, because full production plans were not available. Fortunately, a pattern aircraft was provided by the US Navy in the form of the two-seater Red 13 (originally known as White 35) which was deteriorating after

The two-seater White 35, in the background, together with Tango Tango – the first two flying replicas completed by the Me 262 Project. (Jim Larsen)

<< Bob Hammer with fellow members of the Me 262 Project team.
(Jim Larsen)

< Single-seater Me 262 replica under construction at the Me 262 Project's facility in 2005.
(Me 262 Project)

▲ *Front view of the engine cowling which houses the General Electric J-85 turbojet. (Me 262 Project)*

From 1993 onwards, considerable fabrication and component assembly work took place at the Texas Airplane Factory at Fort Worth, but by 1998 the project was transferred to Everett, Washington, and placed under the leadership of Bob Hammer, a former Boeing engineer. The following year, the airframes and components were transported to new facilities in the Seattle area – Boeing's home town – where Hammer was able to draw upon a high level of expertise to form his team for the final stage of the project. In June 1999 tragedy struck unexpectedly when Snyder was killed in an F-86 Sabre crash in New Jersey. Undaunted, the team continued its work in accordance with the project founder's wishes.

The Me 262 Project is committed to constructing just five airworthy aircraft

years on outdoor display at NAS Willow Grove, Pennsylvania. Snyder struck a deal with the US Navy, and in return for using Red 13 his team would restore it to static display condition.

◄ *White 1, the two-seater Me 262B-1c trainer, being wheeled out ready for flight. (Jim Larsen)*

◀◀ *A magnificent air-to-air shot of a beautiful aircraft – Tango-Tango is now registered in Germany as D-IMTT. (Jim Larsen)*

◀ *Fuselage of Yellow 5 in September 2008, static-display aircraft. (Jim Larsen)*

in three variants with the following designations; one of the A-1c single-seater, two of the B-1c two-seater and two of the A/B-1c 'convertible' variants designed to be readily re-configured between single and two-seater models. During the Second World War, all operational Me 262 s were 'a' models if fitted with the Jumo 004 engine, or experimental 'b' models with the BMW 003 engine. This left 'c' as the next unassigned suffix and has been adopted to denote the new J-85 powerplant. The individual aircraft have also been allocated project names according to their markings, such as White 1 and Tango-Tango.

Restoration of the original template aircraft, Red 13, was completed in late 2000 and it now forms the centrepiece of the indoor display area at the museum at Willow Grove. Meanwhile, the engineers were encountering a series of challenges in creating replica Me 262s, starting with the jet engines. Clearly the Jumo 004 jet was neither available nor desirable and the General Electric J-85, which powers many modern business jets, was selected as its replacement. With 2,850lb of thrust, the J-85 certainly offers more than sufficient thrust to replicate the Me 262's flight characteristics, but visually it bears little

From the beginning there was little interest in creating a plane that only looked like an Me 262; the objective was to create precision duplicates of the jet. There were considerable technical challenges to overcome – surviving airframes were rare and technical drawings were incomplete...

Comments on the origins of the Me 262 project

Did you know?
In comparison with the Me 262's maximum level speed of 560mph (900km/h), a modern combat jet, such as the Eurofighter, flies almost three times faster at around 1,550mph (2,495km/h).

resemblance to the original engines and consequently it was hidden within carefully engineered castings of the Jumos. This also served to maintain the correct engine nacelle weight, as the J-85 is much lighter than its German counterpart. In theory, the new engine is capable of a significant increase in speed and performance, but as the critical concern is to ensure airframe integrity and pilot safety, the new aircraft will not be pushed beyond the 600+mph (970+km/h) range.

This 'no compromise' approach was carried through to all aspects of the construction. While aluminium would have been lighter, they stuck to a steel skin as with the original wartime aircraft which were built at a time of aluminium shortages. Fine details such as the slotted screws were adhered to, and in the same manner the instrument panel and landing-gear doors were fabricated from plywood. The landing gear of the Me 262 was always a notoriously weak area, and several critical improvements have been made to this and to the braking systems.

▼ *White 1, registered in the USA as N262AZ. (Jim Larsen)*

The first of the replicas, the Me 262B-1c two-seater White 1, successfully took to the skies on 2 December 2002 at Paine Field, Seattle, and flew for thirty-five minutes with pilot Wolf Czaia at the controls. Unfortunately, there was a temporary setback the following month when the aircraft was damaged after the left main landing gear collapsed upon landing. Repairs were made and White 1 was soon flying again, and it has since been delivered to its new owner. A second aircraft, the Me 262A/B-1c single-seater Tango-Tango, made its maiden flight on 15 August 2002, and after being shipped to the Messerschmitt Foundation at Manching, Germany it became the star attraction at the 2006 ILA Berlin Air Show. Progress is continuing on the third aircraft, and in 2009 the Me 262 Project team also completed a static-display aircraft known as Gelbe 5 (Yellow 5). This is being offered for sale, and work will proceed with the remaining $2 million flying examples once buyers have been found for these.

The legend continues...

◄ *Completed, the Yellow 5 static-display replica in JG7 colours.* (Jim Larsen)

Did you know?
Clive Cussler's fictional adventurer hero, Dirk Pitt, has his own Me 262 which he uncovered during the excavation of a hidden airfield.

Me 262A-1A *SCHWALBE*

Crew	1	
Wingspan	41ft	12.6m
Length	34ft 9in	10.60m
Height	12ft 7in	3.83m
Wing area	233.3sq ft	21.68sq m
Weight empty	8,820lb	4,000kg
Max. loaded weight	14,930lb	6,770kg
Powerplant	2 x Jumo 004B-1 turbojets, 1,980lb/900kg thrust	
Max. level speed at 7,000m	540–560mph	870–900km/h
Approx. service ceiling	37,500ft	11,400m
Initial rate of climb	3,900ft/min	1,200m/min
Range at 9,000m	650 miles	1,050km
Armament	4 x 30mm MK108 cannon	

Me 262B-1A

Crew	2	
Max level speed at 7,000m	497mph	800km/h

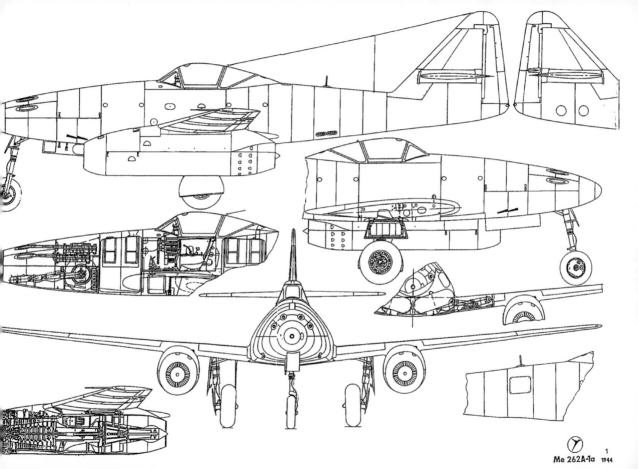

Me 262A-1a 1944

1

➤ *A US serviceman examines an unfinished Me 262 at an underground factory near Kahla. (US National Archives)*

1939

April	Requirements drawn-up for jet-powered fighter
7 June	Projekt 1065 design submitted to RLM
19 December	RLM officials inspect mock-up of Projekt 1065

1940

1 March	Contract issued for three prototypes for flight testing
15 May	Modified design submitted with engines relocated under wings
July	Junkers begins development of Jumo 004 engine
August	First run of BMW 003 jet engine
November	First run of the Jumo 004

1941

January	Prototype Me 262 completed
2 April	Heinkel He 280 flies with HeS 8 turbojet
18 April	First flight of Me 262 V1 (PC-UA) flown with conventional Jumo piston engine as turbojets are not ready
25 July	Order for five experimental Me 262s and twenty pre-production aircraft
25 November	Me 262 V1 flies with BMW 003 jet-engines which fail at take-off

1942

15 March	Jumo 004A jet-engine flight tested beneath a Bf 110
18 July	First all-jet flight of Me 262 V3 (PC-UC), powered by Jumo 004s
2 October	First flight of Me 262 V2 with Jumo 004s
October	Order for forty-five Me 262s to supplement fifteen already ordered

1943

2 March	Me 262 V1 flies for first time solely powered by Jumo 004Bs
24 April	Major General Adolf Galland flies Me262 V4 (PC-UD)
26 June	Me 262 V5 (PC-UE) flies with fixed nose-wheel
17 August	Raid on Regensburg factory destroys Me 262 jigs.
October	Jumo 004B-1 flight tested on Me262
26 November	Me 262 V3 with retractable undercarriage demonstrated to Hitler
December	Me 262 V6 flight tested with pressurised cockpit
12 December	Hitler instructs that the Me 262 should be a fighter-bomber

1944

March	Jägerstab (Fighter Staff) established

April	Erprobungskommando 262 formed at Lager-Lechfeld in Bavaria
	Luftwaffe accepts first pre-production Me 262s
	First operational sorties with Me 262
8 June	Hitler orders production to be restricted almost exclusively to bomber version
July	Start of deliveries of the *Sturmvogel* fighter-bomber
25 July	First kill credited to an Me 262 is an RAF reconnaissance Mosquito
August	First USAAF victory over an Me 262
September	Kommando Nowoty formed
	Kommando Schenk bomber unit formed
October	KG 51 operational
	Hitler orders Me 262 to be built as attack bomber
2 November	R4M rockets deployed in combat
4 November	Me 262 to be produced as a fighter
8 November	Major Nowotny killed
December	Sonderkommando Braunegg reconnaissance unit formed
	10/NJG 11 Kommando Welter formed

1945 _____

| January | Jagdverband 44 formed under Adolf Galland. |

A view of the underside showing the recesses for the two main wheels when retracted.

27 February	Rocket-boosted Me 262C-1a *Heimatschützer I* tested.
1 March	The most concentrated interception ever staged, twenty-five Me 262s attack USAAF bombers over Dresden
25 April	Hans-Guido Mutke lands his Me 262A at Zürich's Dubendorf Military Airfield
8 May	Germany surrenders – the war in Europe is over

2002 _____

2 December	Me 262B-1c two-seater replica White 1 flies at Paine Field, Seattle

2003 _____

15 August	Me 262A/B/B-1c Tango-Tango makes maiden flight

APPENDIX 3: GLOSSARY

ADS	Air Disarmament Squadron (USA)
ATI	Air Technical Intelligence (USA)
BMW	Bayerische Motorenwerke – Bavarian Motor Works
Deichselschlepp	'Air trailer' towed-bomb concept
EKdo	Erprobungskommando – Luftwaffe testing unit
FE	Foreign Equipment – applied to captured enemy aircraft
FuG	Funkgerät – radar equipment
Gruppe	Luftwaffe wing or group
He	Prefix for Heinkel aircraft
JABO	Jagdbomber – fighter-bomber
Jumo	Junkers Motoren – Junkers motor company
Me	Prefix for Messerschmitt aircraft
MK	Maschinenkanone or machine cannon/gun
Nachtjäger	Night-fighter or hunter
NJG	Nachtjägdgeschwader – night-fighter group
RAE	Royal Aircraft Establishment (Farnborough)
RAF	Royal Air Force
RATO	Rocket-Assisted Take-Off
RLM	Reichsluftministerium – German Air Ministry

RfRuK	Reichsministerium für Rüstung und Kriegsproduktion – Reich Ministry for Armament and War Production
Schnellbomber	Fast Bomber
Schwalbe	Swallow
Staffel	Squadron
Sturmvogel	Stormbird
USAAF	United States Army Air Force
USAF	United States Air Force (from 1947)
V	Versuchsmuster – experimental/test

Tango-Tango taxiing at ILA 2008, Berlin. (Jan Honcu)